GRADE 2

Math

Frank Schaffer Publications

D1708716

Table of Contents

Frank Schaffer Publications®

Send all inquiries to:
Frank Schaffer Publications
3195 Wilson Drive NW
Grand Rapids, Michigan 49534

Math—Grade 2

ISBN 0-7696-8222-7

1 2 3 4 5 6 7 8 9 10 WAL 10 09 08 07 06

Classification Fun

Directions: Write each word in the correct row at the bottom of the page.

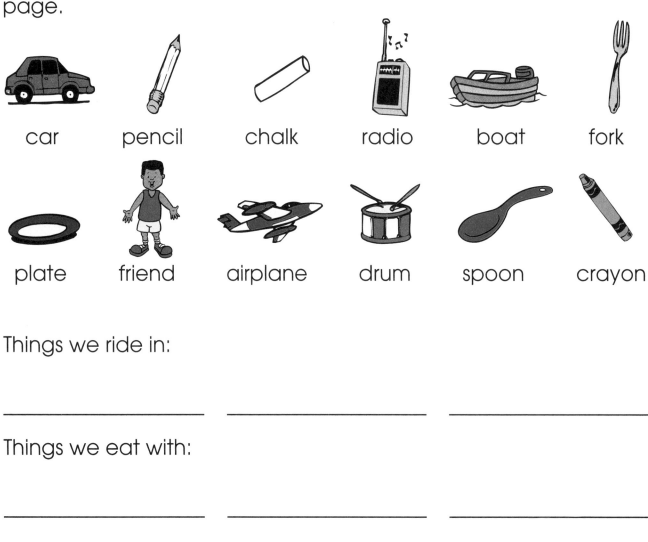

| car | pencil | chalk | radio | boat | fork |

| plate | friend | airplane | drum | spoon | crayon |

Things we ride in:

_____   _____   _____

Things we eat with:

_____   _____   _____

Things we draw with:

_____   _____   _____

Things we listen to:

_____   _____   _____

Clown Capers

Directions: Count the number of each thing in the picture. Write the number on the line.

Dot-to-Dot Fun

Directions: Connect the dots. Color the creature.

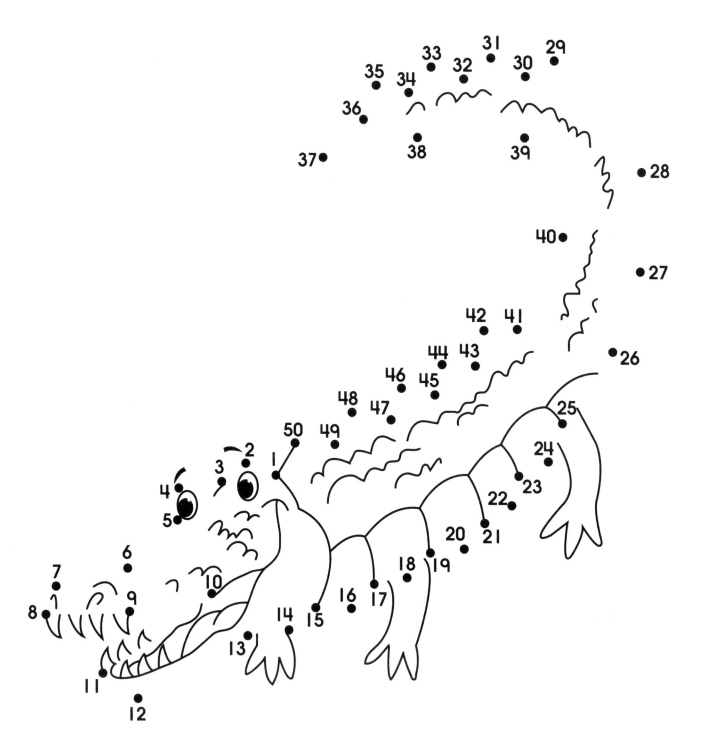

Number Words

Directions: Write each number beside the correct picture. Then, write it again.

one	two	three	four	five	six	seven	eight	nine	ten

Example:

six   six

Sequencing Numbers

Sequencing is putting numbers in the correct order.

Directions: Write the missing numbers.

Example: 4, __5__ ,6

3, _____ , 5   7, _____ , 9   8, _____ , 10

6, _____ , 8   _____ , 3, 4   _____ , 5, 6

5, 6, _____   _____ , 6, 7   _____ , 3, 4

_____ , 9, 10   _____ , 7, 8   2, _____ , 4

2, 3, _____   1, 2, _____   7, 8, _____

2, _____ , 4   _____ , 7, 8   4, _____ , 6

6, 7, _____   2, 3, _____   1, _____ , 3

7, 8, _____   _____ , 3, 4   _____ , 9, 10

Two for the Pool

Directions: Count by **2**s. Write the numbers to **30** in the water drops. Begin at the top of the slide and go down.

Cookie Clues

Directions: Find out what holds something good! Count by **5**s to connect the dots. Color the picture.

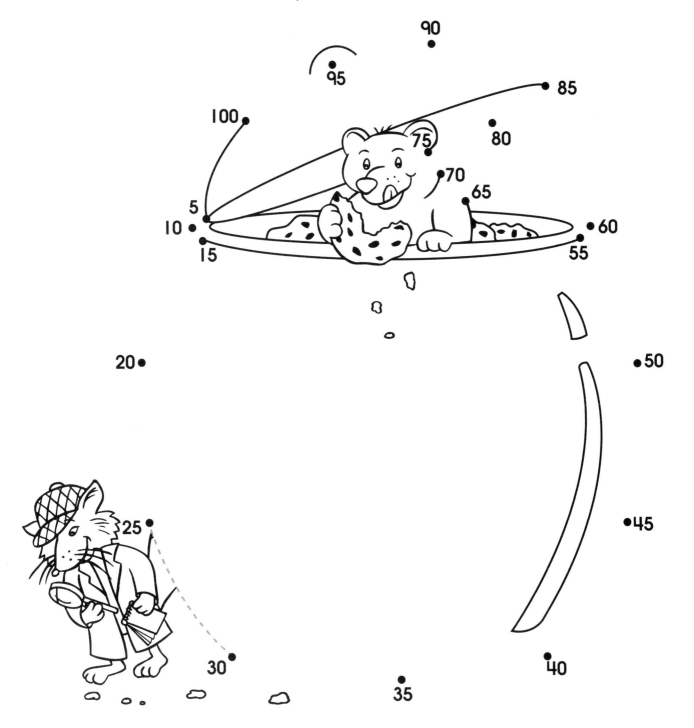

Desert Trek

Directions: Count by **10**s. Color each canteen with a **10** to lead the camel to the watering hole.

"Mouth" Math

Directions: Write < or > in each circle. Make sure the "mouth" is open toward the greater number!

36 ◯ 49   35 ◯ 53

20 ◯ 18   74 ◯ 21

53 ◯ 76   68 ◯ 80

29 ◯ 26   45 ◯ 19

90 ◯ 89   70 ◯ 67

Have a Ball!

Directions: Color the second ball **brown.**

Color the sixth ball yellow.

Color the fourth ball **orange.**

Color the first ball **black.**

Color the fifth ball **green.**

Color the seventh ball **purple.**

Which Place in the Race?

Directions: Write the correct word to tell each runner's place in the race.

How Many Robots in All?

Directions: Look at the pictures. Complete the addition sentences.

Example:

How many s are there in all?

2 + 4 = _6_

How many s are there in all?

3 + 5 = ___

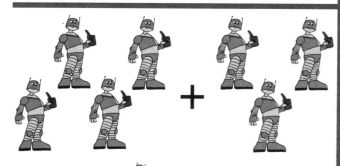

How many s are there in all?

4 + 3 = ___

How many s are there in all?

4 + 1 = ___

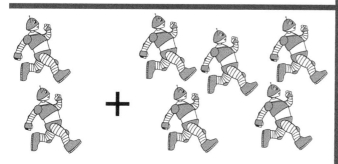

How many s are there in all?

2 + 5 = ___

How many s are there in all?

4 + 4 = ___

15   *Math: Grade 2*

The Missing Chickens

Directions: Draw the missing pictures. Complete the addition sentences.

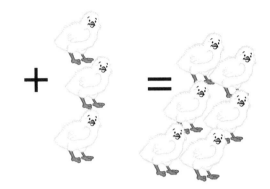

Example:

$\_\_\_ + 2 = 3$

$\_\_\_ + 3 = 6$

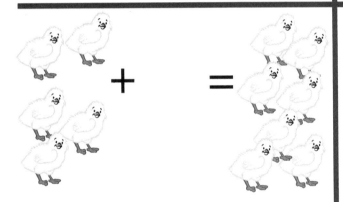

$5 + \_\_\_ = 7$

$\_\_\_ + 3 = 5$

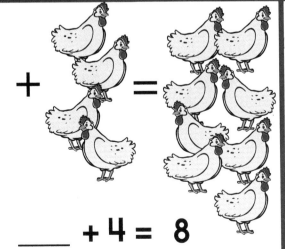

$\_\_\_ + 4 = 8$

$7 + \_\_\_ = 8$

16   *Math: Grade 2*

Counting Up

Directions: Count up to get the sum. Write the missing addend in each blank.

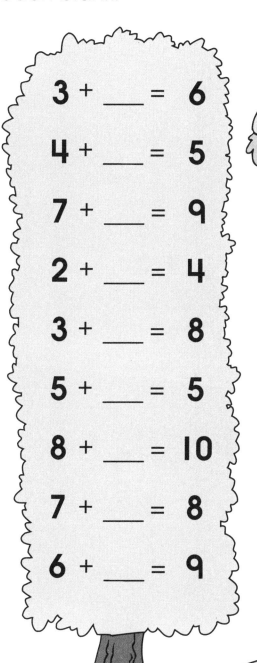

$3 + \underline{\quad} = 6$

$4 + \underline{\quad} = 5$

$7 + \underline{\quad} = 9$

$2 + \underline{\quad} = 4$

$3 + \underline{\quad} = 8$

$5 + \underline{\quad} = 5$

$8 + \underline{\quad} = 10$

$7 + \underline{\quad} = 8$

$6 + \underline{\quad} = 9$

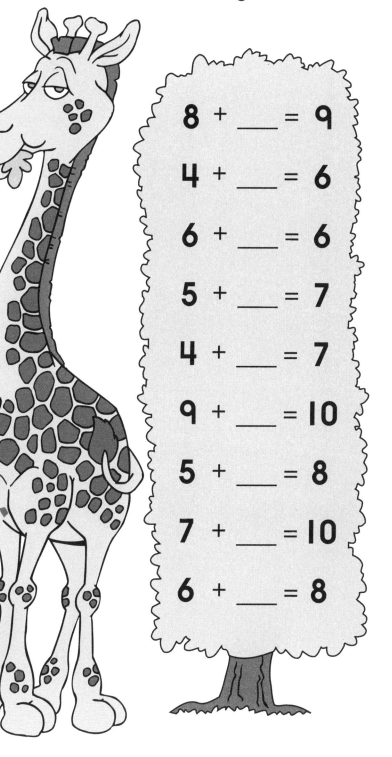

$8 + \underline{\quad} = 9$

$4 + \underline{\quad} = 6$

$6 + \underline{\quad} = 6$

$5 + \underline{\quad} = 7$

$4 + \underline{\quad} = 7$

$9 + \underline{\quad} = 10$

$5 + \underline{\quad} = 8$

$7 + \underline{\quad} = 10$

$6 + \underline{\quad} = 8$

17 *Math: Grade 2*

Coloring by Number

Directions: Find each sum.
If the sum is **13**, color the space **brown.**
If the sum is **14**, color the space yellow.
If the sum is **16**, color the space **red.**
If the sum is **17**, color the space **blue.**

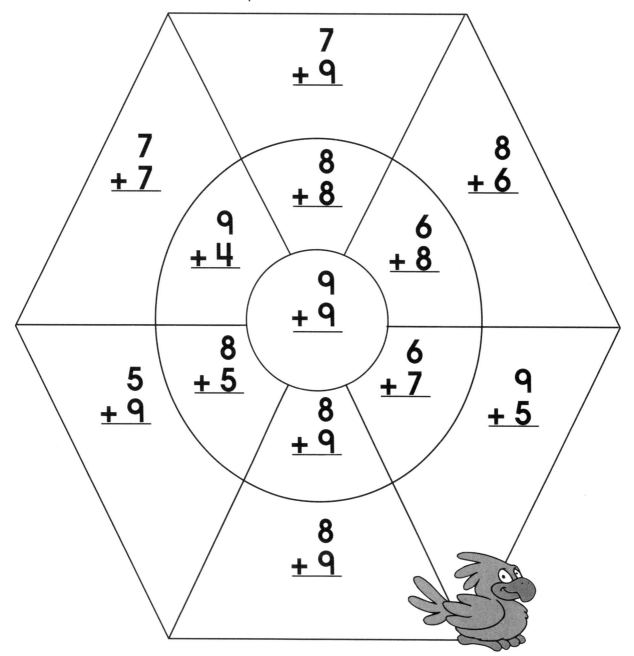

Math: Grade 2

Problem Solving

Directions: Solve each problem.

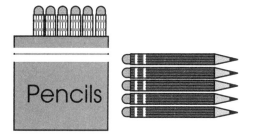

6
+ 5

pencils in a box
more pencils
pencils in all

grapes on a plate
more grapes
grapes in all

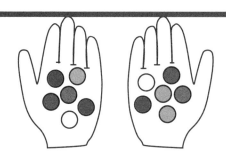

marbles in one hand
marbles in the other hand
marbles in all

people at the table
more people coming in
people in all

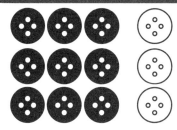

black buttons
white buttons
buttons in all

19 *Math: Grade 2*

Name _____

Hop Along Numbers

Directions: Use the number line to count back.

Example: 8, __7__, __6__

0 1 2 3 4 5 6 7 8 9 10

7 – 3 = ___

7, ___, ___, ___

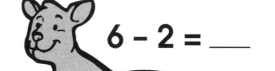

6 – 2 = ___

6, ___, ___

8 – 1 = ___

8, ___

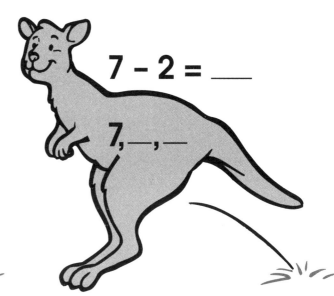

7 – 2 = ___

7, ___, ___

Math: Grade 2

Leaves Leaving the Limb

Directions: Subtract to find the difference. Use the code to color the leaves. Code: **0 = green   1 = red   2 = yellow   3 = brown**

$$\begin{array}{r} 1 \\ -0 \\ \hline \end{array}$$

$$\begin{array}{r} 5 \\ -2 \\ \hline \end{array}$$

$$\begin{array}{r} 3 \\ -3 \\ \hline \end{array}$$

$$\begin{array}{r} 2 \\ -1 \\ \hline \end{array}$$

$$\begin{array}{r} 3 \\ -1 \\ \hline \end{array}$$

$$\begin{array}{r} 2 \\ -2 \\ \hline \end{array}$$

$$\begin{array}{r} 4 \\ -2 \\ \hline \end{array}$$

$$\begin{array}{r} 5 \\ -3 \\ \hline \end{array}$$

$$\begin{array}{r} 3 \\ -0 \\ \hline \end{array}$$

$$\begin{array}{r} 5 \\ -4 \\ \hline \end{array}$$

$$\begin{array}{r} 1 \\ -1 \\ \hline \end{array}$$

$$\begin{array}{r} 2 \\ -1 \\ \hline \end{array}$$

How many of each color?

 _____   _____   _____   _____

         Math: Grade 2

Secrets of Subtraction

Directions: Solve the subtraction problems. Use the code to find the secret message.

Code:

7	5	2	6	4	3
K	T	Y	E	W	A

PLEASE, DON'T EVER

8 -3	10 - 7	9 -2	10 - 4

| ___ | ___ | ___ | ___ |

9 -6	6 - 2	7 -4	8 -6

| ___ | ___ | ___ | ___ |

MY MATH!

Subtraction Fun

Directions: Subtract to find each difference.

10	7	9	8	10
− 5	− 2	− 8	− 4	− 10

8	7	10	9	9
− 3	− 6	− 3	− 7	− 1

9	6	10	8	10
− 6	− 3	− 9	− 5	− 4

Math: Grade 2

Subtraction Facts Through 18

Directions: Subtract.
Example:

$$\begin{array}{r} 15 \\ -\ 7 \\ \hline 8 \end{array}$$

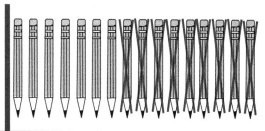

$$\begin{array}{r} 16 \\ -\ 9 \\ \hline \end{array}$$

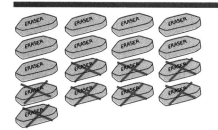

$$\begin{array}{r} 17 \\ -\ 8 \\ \hline \end{array}$$

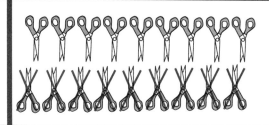

$$\begin{array}{r} 18 \\ -\ 9 \\ \hline \end{array}$$

Directions: Subtract.

18 − 9	13 − 5	16 − 8	17 − 9	14 − 6	13 − 9
17 − 8	15 − 9	14 − 5	13 − 6	16 − 7	12 − 4
14 − 7	15 − 8	16 − 9	12 − 7	15 − 7	13 − 4
15 − 6	14 − 8	12 − 3	13 − 9	14 − 9	11 − 3

24 *Math: Grade 2*

"Grrreat" Picture

Directions: Subtract. Write the answer in the space. Then, color the spaces according to the answers.

1 = white   2 = **purple**   3 = **black**   4 = green   5 = yellow
6 = blue   7 = pink   8 = gray   9 = orange   10 = red

Facts for 10

Directions: Add or subtract.

Examples:

$$\begin{array}{r} 5 \\ +5 \\ \hline 10 \end{array}$$

$$\begin{array}{r} 6 \\ +4 \\ \hline \end{array}$$
$$\begin{array}{r} 4 \\ +6 \\ \hline \end{array}$$

$$\begin{array}{r} 7 \\ +3 \\ \hline \end{array}$$
$$\begin{array}{r} 3 \\ +7 \\ \hline \end{array}$$

$$\begin{array}{r} 10 \\ -5 \\ \hline 5 \end{array}$$

$$\begin{array}{r} 10 \\ -4 \\ \hline \end{array}$$
$$\begin{array}{r} 10 \\ -6 \\ \hline \end{array}$$

$$\begin{array}{r} 10 \\ -3 \\ \hline \end{array}$$
$$\begin{array}{r} 10 \\ -7 \\ \hline \end{array}$$

$$\begin{array}{r} 8 \\ +2 \\ \hline \end{array}$$
$$\begin{array}{r} 2 \\ +8 \\ \hline \end{array}$$

$$\begin{array}{r} 9 \\ +1 \\ \hline \end{array}$$
$$\begin{array}{r} 1 \\ +9 \\ \hline \end{array}$$

$$\begin{array}{r} 10 \\ -2 \\ \hline \end{array}$$
$$\begin{array}{r} 10 \\ -8 \\ \hline \end{array}$$

$$\begin{array}{r} 10 \\ -1 \\ \hline \end{array}$$
$$\begin{array}{r} 10 \\ -9 \\ \hline \end{array}$$

$$\begin{array}{r} 4 \\ +6 \\ \hline \end{array}$$
$$\begin{array}{r} 5 \\ +5 \\ \hline \end{array}$$
$$\begin{array}{r} 9 \\ +1 \\ \hline \end{array}$$
$$\begin{array}{r} 10 \\ -8 \\ \hline \end{array}$$
$$\begin{array}{r} 10 \\ -3 \\ \hline \end{array}$$
$$\begin{array}{r} 10 \\ -0 \\ \hline \end{array}$$

Name _____

Addition and Subtraction Fun

Directions: Solve the number problem under each picture. Write **+** or **–** to show if you should add or subtract.

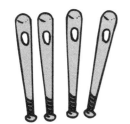

Example:

How many s in all?

$4 + 5 =$ _____ 9

How many  s in all?

$7 \quad 5 =$ _____

Example:

How many s are left?

$12 - 3 =$ _____ 9

How many s are left?

$15 \quad 8 =$ _____

How many s in all?

$5 \quad 8 =$ _____

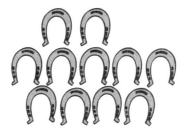

How many s are left?

$11 \quad 4 =$ _____

27 *Math: Grade 2*

Big Families

Directions: Complete each number sentence in each number family.

2
0 + ___ = 2
2 + 0 = ___
___ − 0 = 2
2 − 2 = ___

3
1 + 2 = ___
___ + 1 = 3
3 − ___ = 2
3 − 2 = ___

4
___ + 3 = 4
3 + 1 = ___
4 − ___ = 3
___ − 3 = 1

5
2 + 3 = ___
___ + 2 = 5
5 − ___ = 3
___ − 3 = 2

6
2 + ___ = 6
4 + 2 = ___
6 − ___ = 4
6 − 4 = ___

6
5 + ___ = 6
___ + ___ = ___
6 − ___ = 5
___ − 5 = ___

 Math: Grade 2

Place Value: Ones, Tens

The **place value** of a digit or numeral is shown by where it is in the number. For example, in the number **23, 2** has the place value of **tens**, and **3** is **ones**.

Directions: Add the tens and ones and write your answers in the blanks.

Example:

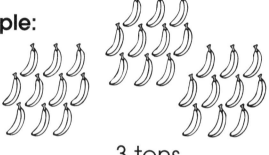

3 tens   +   3 ones   =   __33__

	tens ones			tens ones
7 tens + 5 ones	= _____	4 tens + 0 ones	= _____
2 tens + 3 ones	= _____	8 tens + 1 one	= _____
5 tens + 2 ones	= _____	1 ten + 1 one	= _____
5 tens + 4 ones	= _____	6 tens + 3 ones	= _____
9 tens + 5 ones	= _____		

Directions: Draw a line to the correct number.

6 tens + 7 ones   73

4 tens + 2 ones   67

8 tens + 0 ones   51

7 tens + 3 ones   80

5 tens + 1 one   42

   29   *Math: Grade 2*

Numbers 11 Through 18

1¢   10¢   10¢

Directions: Complete the problems.

Example:

  ___ten___one = ___

  ___ten___ones = ___

  ___ten___ones = ___

  ___ten___ones = ___

  ___ten___ones = ___

  ___ten___ones = ___

  ___ten___ones = ___

  ___ten___ones = ___

 Math: Grade 2

Numbers 40 Through 99

Directions: Complete the problems.

Example:

__4__ tens __5__ ones = __45__

_____ tens _____ ones = _____

_____ tens = _____

_____ tens _____ ones = _____

_____ tens _____ ones = _____

_____ tens _____ ones = _____

_____ tens = _____

_____ tens _____ ones = _____

Hundreds, Tens, and Ones

Directions: Count the groups of crayons. Write the number of hundreds, tens, and ones.

Example:

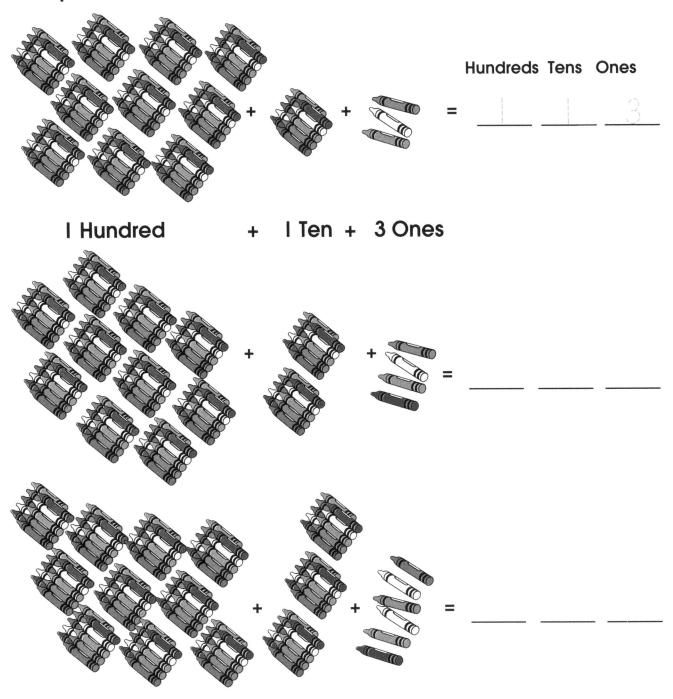

Hundreds Tens Ones

1 Hundred + 1 Ten + 3 Ones

Count 'Em Up!

Directions: Look at the example. Then, write the missing numbers in the blanks.

Example:

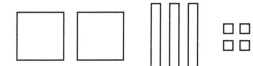

2 hundreds + 3 tens + 6 ones =

hundreds	tens	ones	
2	3	6	= 236

	hundreds	tens	ones	
3 hundreds + 4 tens + 8 ones =	3	4	8	= _____
___ hundreds + ___ ten + ___ ones =	2	1	7	= _____
___ hundreds + ___ tens + ___ ones =	6	3	5	= _____
___ hundreds + ___ tens + ___ ones =	4	7	9	= _____
___ hundreds + ___ tens + ___ ones =	2	9	4	= _____
___ hundreds + ___ tens + ___ ones =	4	2	0	= _____
3 hundreds + 1 ten + 3 ones = _____				= _____
3 hundreds + ___ tens + 7 ones = _____		5		= _____
6 hundreds + 2 tens + ___ ones = _____			8	= _____

Place Value: Thousands

Directions: Study the example. Write the missing numbers.

Example:

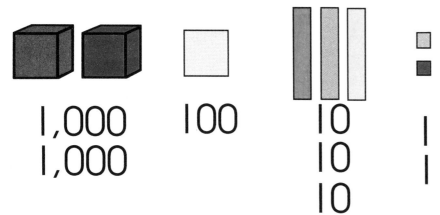

1,000   100   10   1
1,000   10   1
                10

2 thousands + 1 hundred + __3__ tens + 2 ones = __2,132__

5,286 = ____ thousands + ____ hundreds + ____ tens + ____ ones

1,831 = ____ thousand + ____ hundreds + ____ tens + ____ one

8,972 = ____ thousands + ____ hundreds + ____ tens + ____ ones

4,528 = ____ thousands + ____ hundreds + ____ tens + ____ ones

3,177 = ____ thousands + ____ hundred + ____ tens + ____ ones

Directions: Draw a line to the number that has:

8 hundreds	7,103
5 ones	2,862
9 tens	5,996
7 thousands	1,485

 Math: Grade 2

Adding Tens

```
  3 tens        30              6 tens        60
+ 4 tens      + 40            + 2 tens      + 20
  7 tens        70              8 tens        80
```

Directions: Add.

```
  2 tens        20              6 tens        60
+ 4 tens      + 40            + 2 tens      + 20
    tens                          tens
```

```
  20       10       40       30       50
+ 20     + 50     + 20     + 40     + 30
```

```
  30       60       20       70       10
+ 20     + 10     + 50     + 10     + 10
```

```
  10       40       80       60       20
+ 20     + 40     + 10     + 30     + 60
```

```
  70       40       30       50       30
+ 20     + 10     + 10     + 40     + 30
```

2-Digit Addition

Directions: Study the example. Follow the steps to add.

Example:

```
  33
+41
```

Step 1: Add the ones.

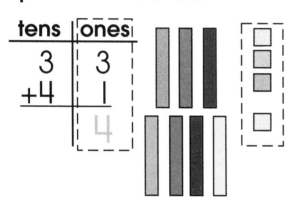

tens	ones
3	3
+4	1
	4

tens	ones
4	2
+2	4
6	6

Step 2: Add the tens.

tens	ones
3	3
+4	1
7	4

tens	ones
5	0
+4	7
9	7

```
  24        15        38        11        37        72        33        10
+62       +23       +61       +26       +42       +11       +51       +30
```

```
  25        62        32        25        82        91        16        55
+42       +14       +44       +13       + 6       + 5       +71       + 3
```

36 *Math: Grade 2*

Name _____

Prehistoric Problems

Directions: Solve the subtraction problems. Use the code to color the picture.

Code: **25** = blue   **57** = green
       31 = yellow   **14** = orange
       21 = brown   **11** = red

```
  52
- 21
-----
```

```
  47
- 22
-----
```

```
  25
- 11
-----
```

```
  62
- 31
-----
```

```
  77
- 20
-----
```

```
  51
- 40
-----
```

```
  98
- 41
-----
```

```
  55
- 34
-----
```

```
  69
- 12
-----
```

Math: Grade 2

Name _____

2-Digit Addition

Directions: Add the ones.   Rename 15 as 10 + 5.   Add the tens.

$$
\begin{array}{r} 5\,6 \\ +\,2\,9 \\ \hline \end{array}
\qquad
\begin{array}{r} 6 \\ +\ 9 \\ \hline 15 \text{ or } 10+5 \end{array}
\qquad
\begin{array}{r} 1\ \ \\ 5\,6 \\ +\,2\,9 \\ \hline 5 \end{array}
\qquad
\begin{array}{r} 1\ \ \\ 5\,6 \\ +\,2\,9 \\ \hline 8\,5 \end{array}
$$

Directions: Add the ones.   Rename 12 as 10 + 2.   Add the tens.

$$
\begin{array}{r} 4\,7 \\ +\,3\,5 \\ \hline \end{array}
\qquad
\begin{array}{r} 7 \\ +\ 5 \\ \hline 12 \text{ or } 10+2 \end{array}
\qquad
\begin{array}{r} 1\ \ \\ 4\,7 \\ +\,3\,5 \\ \hline 2 \end{array}
\qquad
\begin{array}{r} 1\ \ \\ 4\,7 \\ +\,3\,5 \\ \hline 8\,2 \end{array}
$$

Directions: Add.

Examples:

$$
\begin{array}{r} 4\,5 \\ +\,2\,8 \\ \hline 7\,3 \end{array}
\qquad
\begin{array}{r} 1\,3 \\ +\,1\,9 \\ \hline 3\,2 \end{array}
\qquad
\begin{array}{r} 4\,8 \\ +\,3\,5 \\ \hline \end{array}
\qquad
\begin{array}{r} 6\,9 \\ +\,1\,8 \\ \hline \end{array}
\qquad
\begin{array}{r} 5\,4 \\ +\,3\,9 \\ \hline \end{array}
$$

$$
\begin{array}{r} 4\,4 \\ +\,1\,7 \\ \hline \end{array}
\qquad
\begin{array}{r} 3\,7 \\ +\,1\,8 \\ \hline \end{array}
\qquad
\begin{array}{r} 2\,8 \\ +\,3\,6 \\ \hline \end{array}
\qquad
\begin{array}{r} 7\,3 \\ +\,1\,8 \\ \hline \end{array}
\qquad
\begin{array}{r} 6\,6 \\ +\,2\,9 \\ \hline \end{array}
$$

$$
\begin{array}{r} 5\,2 \\ +\,3\,9 \\ \hline \end{array}
\qquad
\begin{array}{r} 3\,8 \\ +\,4\,7 \\ \hline \end{array}
\qquad
\begin{array}{r} 6\,4 \\ +\,1\,8 \\ \hline \end{array}
\qquad
\begin{array}{r} 2\,9 \\ +\,4\,5 \\ \hline \end{array}
\qquad
\begin{array}{r} 7\,5 \\ +\,1\,7 \\ \hline \end{array}
$$

38   *Math: Grade 2*

2-Digit Subtraction: Regrouping

Subtraction is "taking away" or subtracting one number from another to find the difference. Regrouping is using **one ten** to form **ten ones, one 100** to form **ten tens,** and so on.

Directions: Study the examples. Follow the steps to subtract.

Example:

```
  37
- 19
```

Step 1:
Regroup.

Step 2:
Subtract the ones.

Step 3:
Subtract the tens.

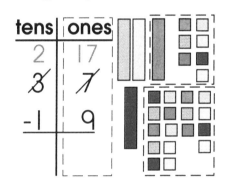

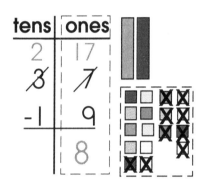

tens	ones
2	17
3̶	7̶
-1	9

tens	ones
2	17
3̶	7̶
-1	9
	8

tens	ones
2	17
3̶	7̶
-1	9
1	8

tens	ones
0	12
1̶	2̶
-	9
	3

tens	ones
2	14
3̶	4̶
-1	6
1	8

tens	ones
3	15
4̶	5̶
-2	9
1	6

```
  28      46      12      30      52      47      21      45
- 19    - 18    -  8    - 12    - 25    - 35    - 13    - 25
```

Addition and Subtraction Review

Directions: Add.

4 + 9	8 + 6	9 + 8	7 + 6	5 + 7	6 + 5
9 + 6	5 + 8	7 + 4	9 + 9	8 + 7	7 + 9
30 + 40	20 + 30	45 + 23	52 + 23	60 + 25	83 + 15

Directions: Subtract.

16 − 7	15 − 9	13 − 4	12 − 7	11 − 9	17 − 8
18 − 9	17 − 9	16 − 8	15 − 8	4 − 7	16 − 9
40 − 30	60 − 10	85 − 23	73 − 41	96 − 43	54 − 44

Adding Hundreds

Examples:

```
  5 hundreds        5 0 0        4 hundreds        4 0 0
+ 3 hundreds      + 3 0 0      + 5 hundreds      + 5 0 0
  8 hundreds        8 0 0        9 hundreds        9 0 0
```

Directions: Add.

```
  3 hundreds        3 0 0        6 hundreds        6 0 0
+ 1 hundreds      + 1 0 0      + 2 hundreds      + 2 0 0
  4 hundreds        4 0 0          hundreds
```

```
  2 0 0             1 0 0          6 0 0             4 0 0
+ 2 0 0           + 7 0 0        + 3 0 0           + 5 0 0
```

```
  3 0 0             8 0 0          4 0 0             7 0 0
+ 4 0 0           + 1 0 0        + 4 0 0           + 2 0 0
```

```
  5 0 0             1 0 0          5 0 0             3 0 0
+ 1 0 0           + 6 0 0        + 2 0 0           + 2 0 0
```

```
  3 0 0             4 0 0          3 0 0             2 0 0
+ 3 0 0           + 2 0 0        + 5 0 0           + 1 0 0
```

3-Digit Addition

```
  2 4 5              2 4 5              2 4 5
+ 2 5 3            + 2 5 3            + 2 5 3
      8                9 8            4 9 8
```

Directions: Add.

Example:

```
  7 4 5                    6 2 3
+   2 3                  + 1 5 6
7 6 8
```

— Add the ones.
— Add the tens.
— Add the hundreds.

— Add the ones.
— Add the tens.
— Add the hundreds.

```
  4 1 5        5 6 6        3 7 3        1 6 0
+ 3 4 2      +   3 3      + 2 2 1      + 3 3 4
```

```
  8 3 5        6 4 2        2 8 7        7 2 3
+   4 2      + 2 5 1      + 4 1 2      +   4 5
```

```
  1 3 3        4 5 4        3 1 4        6 5 4
+ 5 2 2      + 3 2 4      + 6 0 2      + 2 3 5
```

42 *Math: Grade 2*

Subtracting Hundreds

8 hundreds	8 0 0	6 hundreds	6 0 0
− 3 hundreds	− 3 0 0	− 2 hundreds	− 2 0 0
5 hundreds	5 0 0	4 hundreds	400

Directions: Subtract.

Example:

9 hundreds	9 0 0	3 hundreds	3 0 0
− 7 hundreds	− 7 0 0	− 1 hundreds	− 1 0 0
2 hundreds	200	hundreds	

7 0 0	5 0 0	9 0 0	8 0 0
− 3 0 0	− 4 0 0	− 4 0 0	− 5 0 0

6 0 0	3 0 0	5 0 0	4 0 0
− 5 0 0	− 2 0 0	− 1 0 0	− 2 0 0

9 0 0	8 0 0	6 0 0	5 0 0
− 1 0 0	− 4 0 0	− 2 0 0	− 3 0 0

4 0 0	7 0 0	8 0 0	9 0 0
− 1 0 0	− 6 0 0	− 2 0 0	− 6 0 0

Problem Solving

Directions: Solve each problem.

Example:

The grocery store buys 568 cans of beans.

It sells 345 cans of beans.

How many cans of beans are left?

$$\begin{array}{r} 568 \\ -\ 345 \\ \hline 223 \end{array}$$

The cooler holds 732 gallons of milk.

It has 412 gallons of milk in it.

How many more gallons of milk
will it take to fill the cooler?

Ann does 635 push-ups.

Carl does 421 push-ups.

How many more push-ups does Ann do?

Kurt has 386 pennies.

Neal has 32 pennies.

How many more pennies does Kurt have?

It takes 874 nails to build a tree house.

Jillian has 532 nails.

How many more nails does she need?

Multiplication

Multiplication is a short way to find the sum of adding the same number a certain amount of times. For example, 7 x 4 = 28 instead of 7 + 7 + 7 + 7 = 28.

Directions: Study the example. Solve the problems.

Example:

3 + 3 + 3 = 9
3 threes = 9
3 x 3 = 9

7 + 7 = ____
2 sevens = ____
2 x 7 = ____

4 + 4 + 4 + 4 = ____
4 fours = ____
4 x ____ = ____

5 + 5 = ____
2 fives = ____
2 x ____ = ____

2 + 2 + 2 + 2 = ____
4 twos = ____
4 x ____ = ____

6 + 6 = ____
2 sixes = ____
2 x ____ = ____

45 *Math: Grade 2*

Multiplication

Directions: Solve the problems.

9 + 9 = ____

7 + 7 = ____

2 nines = ____

2 sevens = ____

2 x 9 = ____

2 x ____ = ____

4 + 4 + 4 + 4 = ____

8 + 8 + 8 + 8 + 8 = ____

____ fours = ____

____ eights = ____

____ x 4 = ____

____ x 8 = ____

5 + 5 + 5 = ____

9 + 9 = ____

6 + 6 + 6 = ____

____ fives = ____

____ nines = ____

____ sixes = ____

____ x 5 = ____

____ x 9 = ____

____ x 6 = ____

3 + 3 = ____

7 + 7 + 7 + 7 = ____

2 + 2 = ____

____ threes = ____

____ sevens = ____

____ twos = ____

____ x 3 = ____

____ x 7 = ____

____ x 2 = ____

Multiplication

Directions: Use the code to color the fish.

If the answer is:

 6, color it **red.**

 12, color it orange.

 16, color it blue.

 27, color it **brown.**

 8, color it yellow.

 15, color it green.

 18, color it **purple.**

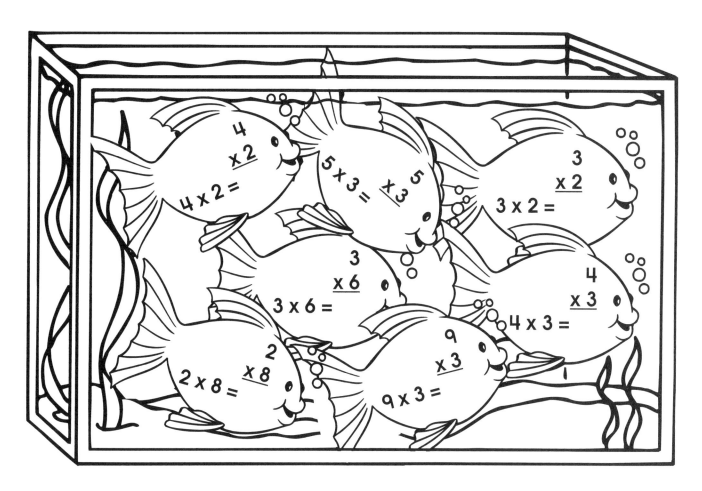

Problem Solving

Directions: Tell if you add, subtract, or multiply. Then, write the answers. Hints: "In all" means to add. "Left" means to subtract. Groups with the same number in each means to multiply.

Example:

There are 6 red birds and 7 blue birds. How many birds in all?

____add____ ___13___ birds

The pet store had 25 goldfish, but 10 were sold. How many goldfish are left?

_____ _____ goldfish

There are 5 cages of bunnies. There are two bunnies in each cage. How many bunnies are there in the store?

_____ _____ bunnies

The store had 18 puppies this morning. It sold 7 puppies today. How many puppies are left?

_____ _____ puppies

Geometry

Geometry is mathematics that has to do with lines and shapes.

Directions: Color the shapes.

Color the triangles blue.
Color the circles **red.**
Color the squares green.
Color the rectangles pink.

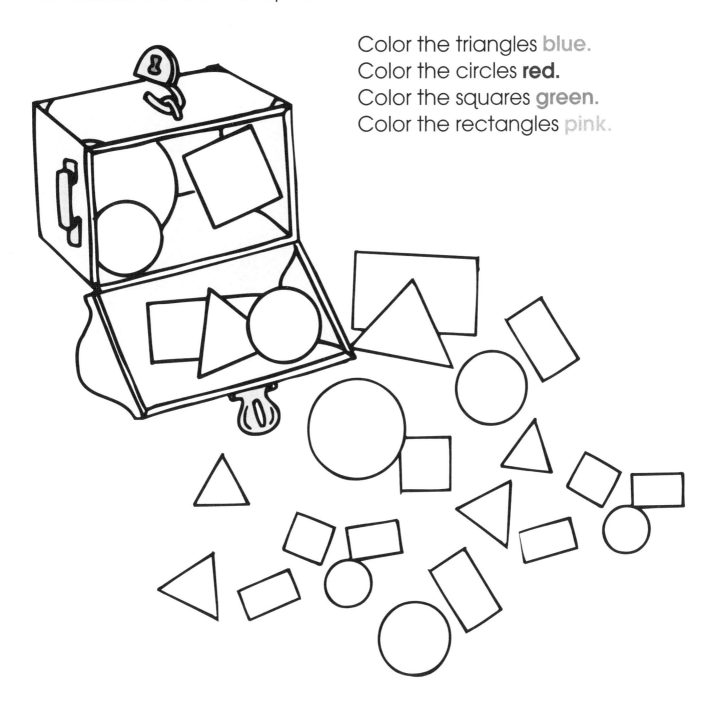

Shapes

Directions: Look at the grid below. All the shapes have straight sides, like a square.

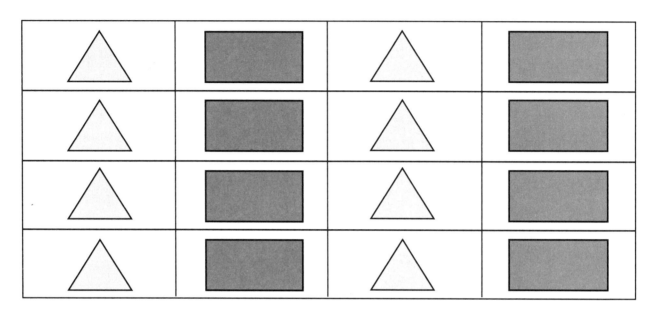

Directions: Now, make your own pattern grid. Use only shapes with straight sides like the grid above. The grid has been started for you.

Measurement: Inches

An **inch** is a unit of length in the standard measurement system.

Directions: Use the ruler on pg. 203 to measure each object to the nearest inch.

Example: The paper clip is about 1 inch long.

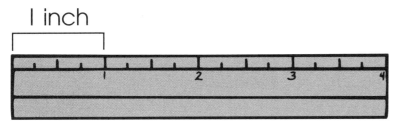

   about __1__ inches

   about _____ inches

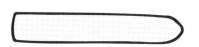   about _____ inches

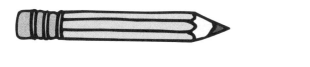   about _____ inches

   about _____ inches

   about _____ inches

about _____ inches

Name _____

Measuring in Centimeters

Directions: Use a centimeter ruler to find the height or the length of the objects below. Write the answer in each blank.

Example:

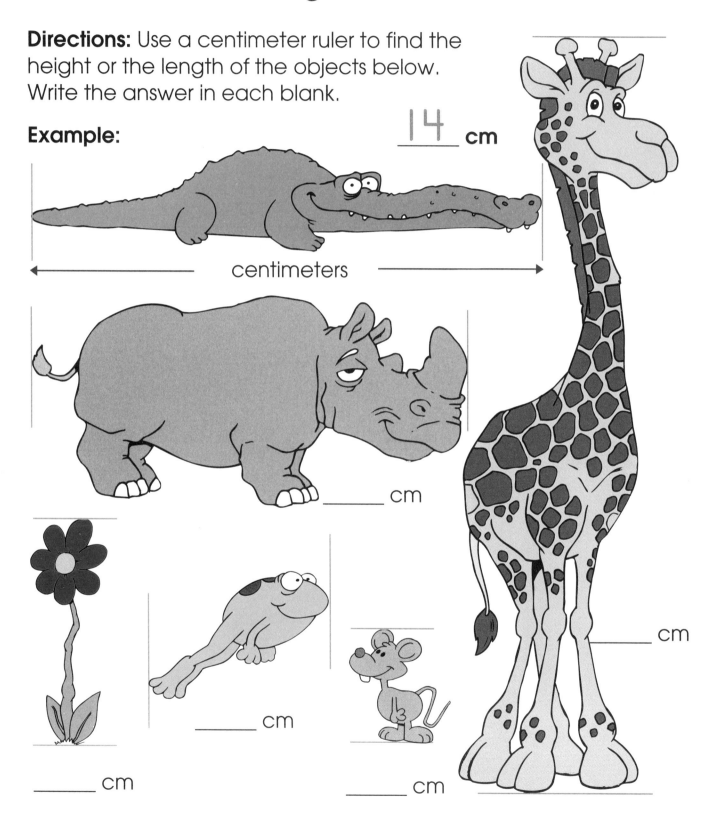

14 cm

centimeters

_____ cm

_____ cm

_____ cm

_____ cm

_____ cm

Name _____

What a Meal!

Directions: Use the pictograph to complete each sentence below.

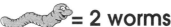 = 2 worms

Grace Goldfish	
Willie Walleye	
Calvin Catfish	
Benny Bluegill	
Beth Bass	
Patty Perch	

1. _____ got the fewest worms.

2. _____ got the most worms.

3. _____ and _____ got the same number of worms.

4. Benny and Patty together caught the same number of worms

 as _____ .

5. Write the number of worms that each fish ate.

_____ _____ _____ _____ _____ _____
   Grace   Willie   Calvin   Benny   Beth   Patty

Graphs

Directions: Count the banana peels in each column. Color the boxes to show how many bananas have been eaten by the monkeys.

Example:

10		10		10		10		10	
9		9		9		9		9	
8		8		8		8		8	
7		7		7		7		7	
6		6		6		6		6	
5		5		5		5		5	
4		4		4		4		4	
3		3		3		3		3	
2		2		2		2		2	
1		1		1		1		1	

Treasure Quest

Directions: Read the directions. Draw the pictures where they belong on the grid. Start at 0 and go . . .

over 2, up 5. Draw a

over 9, up 3. Draw a

over 8, up 6. Draw a

over 5, up 2. Draw a

over 1, up 7. Draw a

over 7, up 1. Draw a

over 6, up 4. Draw a

over 2, up 3. Draw a

over 3, up 1. Draw a

over 4, up 6. Draw a

```
8 | | | | | | | | | | |
7 | | | | | | | | | | |
6 | | | | | | | | | | |
5 | | | | | | | | | | |
4 | | | | | | | | | | |
3 | | | | | | | | | | |
2 | | | | | | | | | | |
1 | | | | | | | | | | |
  0   1   2   3   4   5   6   7   8   9  10
```

Math: Grade 2

Thirds and Fourths

Directions: Each shape has **3** equal parts. Color one section, or $\frac{1}{3}$, of each shape.

Directions: Each shape has **4** equal parts. Color one section, or $\frac{1}{4}$, of each shape.

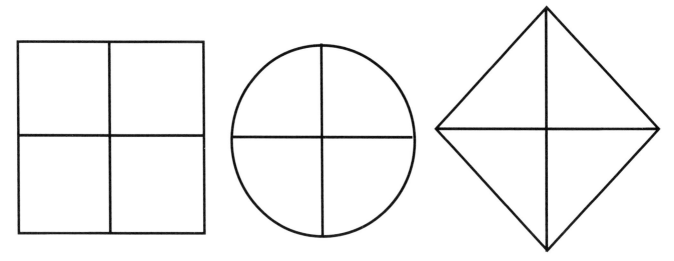

56 *Math: Grade 2*

Name _____

Fractions: Half, Third, Fourth

Directions: Color the correct fraction of each shape.

Examples:

shaded part   1
equal parts   2
$\frac{1}{2}$ (one-half)

shaded part   1
equal parts   3
$\frac{1}{3}$ (one-third)

shaded part   1
equal parts   4
$\frac{1}{4}$ (one-fourth)

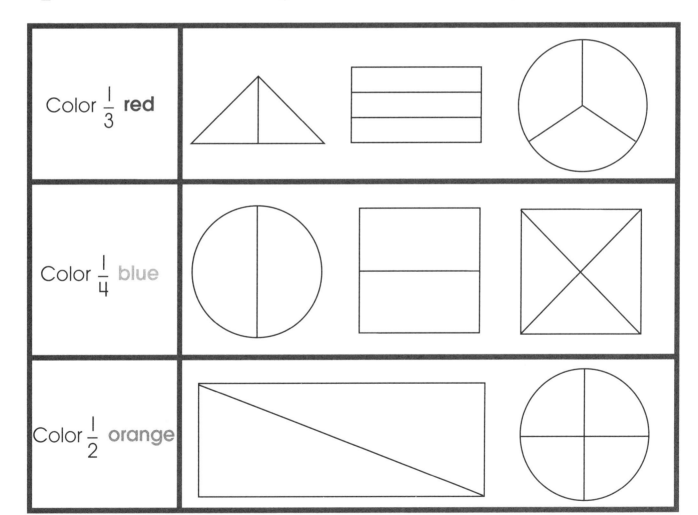

Color $\frac{1}{3}$ **red**

Color $\frac{1}{4}$ blue

Color $\frac{1}{2}$ orange

Math: Grade 2

Fractions: Half, Third, Fourth

Directions: Study the examples. Circle the fraction that shows the shaded part. Then, circle the fraction that shows the white part.

Examples:

shaded	white
$\frac{1}{4}$ $\frac{1}{3}$ $\boxed{\frac{1}{2}}$	$\frac{1}{3}$ $\boxed{\frac{1}{2}}$ $\frac{1}{4}$

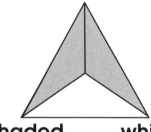

shaded	white
$\frac{1}{2}$ $\boxed{\frac{2}{3}}$ $\frac{3}{4}$	$\frac{2}{3}$ $\frac{1}{2}$ $\boxed{\frac{1}{3}}$

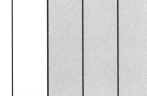

shaded	white
$\frac{1}{4}$ $\frac{1}{2}$ $\boxed{\frac{3}{4}}$	$\boxed{\frac{1}{4}}$ $\frac{2}{3}$ $\frac{1}{2}$

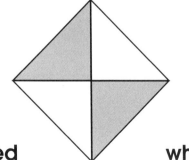

shaded   **white**

$\frac{1}{4}$ $\frac{1}{3}$ $\frac{1}{2}$ $\frac{2}{4}$ $\frac{2}{3}$ $\frac{2}{2}$

shaded   **white**

$\frac{3}{4}$ $\frac{1}{3}$ $\frac{3}{2}$ $\frac{1}{2}$ $\frac{1}{4}$ $\frac{1}{3}$

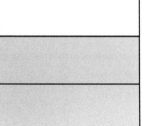

shaded   **white**

$\frac{2}{3}$ $\frac{2}{4}$ $\frac{2}{2}$ $\frac{1}{3}$ $\frac{2}{4}$ $\frac{2}{2}$

shaded   **white**

$\frac{1}{3}$ $\frac{2}{3}$ $\frac{2}{2}$ $\frac{1}{2}$ $\frac{1}{4}$ $\frac{1}{3}$

58   *Math: Grade 2*

Writing the Time

An hour is sixty minutes long. It takes an hour for the BIG HAND to go around the clock. When the BIG HAND is on 12, and the little hand points to a number, that is the hour!

Directions: The **BIG HAND** is on the **12**. Color it **red**. The **little hand** is on the **8**. Color it blue.

The **BIG HAND** is on _____ .

The **little hand** is on _____ .

It is _____ o'clock.

Name _____

Writing the Time

Directions: Color the little hour hand **red**. Fill in the blanks.

The **BIG HAND** is on _____ .

The **little hand** is on _____ .

It is _____ o'clock.

The **BIG HAND** is on _____ .

The **little hand** is on _____ .

It is _____ o'clock.

The **BIG HAND** is on _____ .

The **little hand** is on _____ .

It is _____ o'clock.

The **BIG HAND** is on _____ .

The **little hand** is on _____ .

It is _____ o'clock.

Matching Digital and Face Clocks

Long ago, there were only wind-up clocks. Today, we also have electric and battery clocks. We may soon have solar clocks!

Directions: Match the digital and face clocks that show the same time.

61   *Math: Grade 2*

Writing Time on the Half-Hour

Directions: Write the times.

_____

_____ minutes past

_____

_____ o'clock

_____

_____ minutes past

_____

_____ o'clock

What is your dinner time?

Directions: Circle the time you eat.

Name _____

Counting Pennies

Directions: Count the pennies. How many cents?

Example:

    = **4¢**

        =

     =

        =

  =

   =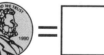

       =

  =

         =

Math: Grade 2

Name _____

Nickels: Counting by Fives

Directions: Count the nickels by 5s. Write the amount.

Example:

5 cents = 1 nickel

   15 ¢

    ¢

Count __5__, __10__, __15__.

Count ____, ____.

 ¢

    ¢

Count ____, ____, ____,

____, ____.

Count ____, ____, ____,

____, ____.

 ¢

    ¢

Count ____, ____, ____,

____.

Count ____, ____, ____,

____, ____, ____.

Math: Grade 2

Dimes: Counting by Tens

Directions: Count by 10s. Write the number. Circle the group with more.

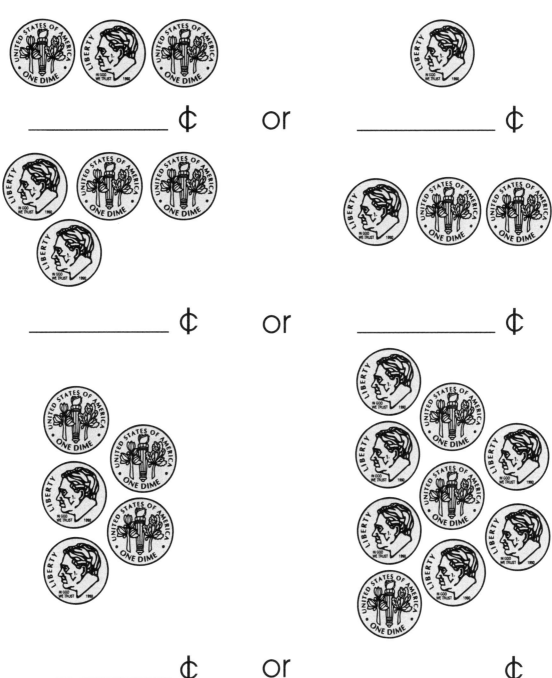

_____ ¢   or   _____ ¢

_____ ¢   or   _____ ¢

_____ ¢   or   _____ ¢

Name _____

Counting With Dimes, Nickels, and Pennies

Directions: Count the money. Start with the dime. Write the amount.

1.

_____ ¢

2.

_____ ¢

3.　Circle the answer.
　　Who has more money?

Counting With Quarters, Dimes, Nickels, and Pennies

Directions: Match the money with the amount.

35 ¢

36 ¢

40 ¢

27 ¢

15 ¢

21 ¢

8 ¢

Making Exact Amounts of Money: Two Ways to Pay

Directions: Find two ways to pay. Show what coins you use.

27¢

1.

_____ quarters

_____ dimes

_____ nickels

_____ pennies

2.

_____ quarters

_____ dimes

_____ nickels

_____ pennies

32¢

3.

_____ quarters

_____ dimes

_____ nickels

_____ pennies

4.

_____ quarters

_____ dimes

_____ nickels

_____ pennies

Making Exact Amounts of Money: How Much More?

Directions: Count the coins. Find out how much more money you need to pay the exact amount.

How much money do you have?   _____ ¢

How much more money do you need?   _____ ¢

How much money do you have?   _____ ¢

How much more money do you need?   _____ ¢

Solve this puzzle.

How much more money
does Monkey need?

_____ ¢

Answer Key

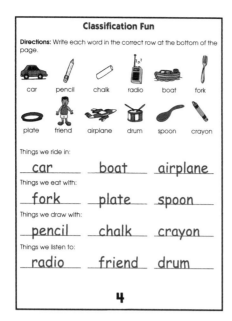

Classification Fun

Directions: Write each word in the correct row at the bottom of the page.

car pencil chalk radio boat fork
plate friend airplane drum spoon crayon

Things we ride in:
car boat airplane

Things we eat with:
fork plate spoon

Things we draw with:
pencil chalk crayon

Things we listen to:
radio friend drum

4

Clown Capers

Directions: Count the number of each thing in the picture. Write the number on the line.

1
2
3
4
5
6
7
8
9
10

5

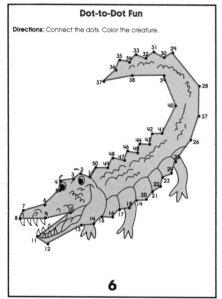

Dot-to-Dot Fun

Directions: Connect the dots. Color the creature.

6

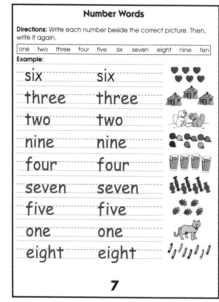

Number Words

Directions: Write each number beside the correct picture. Then, write it again.

one two three four five six seven eight nine ten

Example:

six six
three three
two two
nine nine
four four
seven seven
five five
one one
eight eight

7

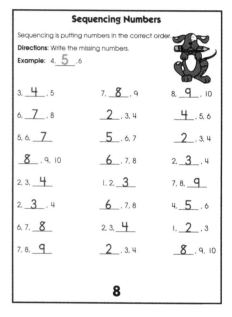

Sequencing Numbers

Sequencing is putting numbers in the correct order.

Directions: Write the missing numbers.

Example: 4, 5, 6

3, 4, 5   7, 8, 9   8, 9, 10
6, 7, 8   2, 3, 4   4, 5, 6
5, 6, 7   5, 6, 7   2, 3, 4
8, 9, 10   6, 7, 8   2, 3, 4
2, 3, 4   1, 2, 3   7, 8, 9
2, 3, 4   6, 7, 8   4, 5, 6
6, 7, 8   2, 3, 4   1, 2, 3
7, 8, 9   2, 3, 4   8, 9, 10

8

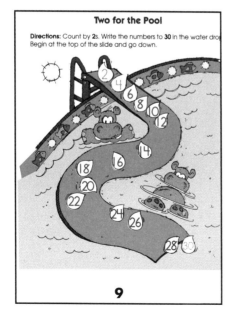

Two for the Pool

Directions: Count by **2s**. Write the numbers to **30** in the water drops. Begin at the top of the slide and go down.

2 4 6 8 10 12 14 16 18 20 22 24 26 28 30

9

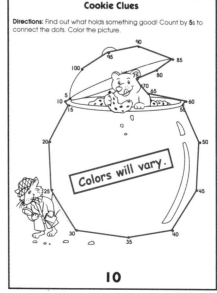

Cookie Clues

Directions: Find out what holds something good! Count by **5s** to connect the dots. Color the picture.

Colors will vary.

10

Math: Grade 2

Desert Trek

Directions: Count by 10s. Color each canteen with a 10 to lead the camel to the watering hole.

11

"Mouth" Math

Directions: Write < or > in each circle. Make sure the "mouth" is open toward the greater number!

36 < 49   35 < 53

20 > 18   74 > 21

53 < 76   68 < 80

29 > 26   45 > 19

90 > 89   70 > 67

12

Have a Ball!

Directions: Color the second ball brown.

Color the sixth ball yellow.

Color the fourth ball orange.

Color the first ball **black.**

Color the fifth ball green.

Color the seventh ball **purple.**

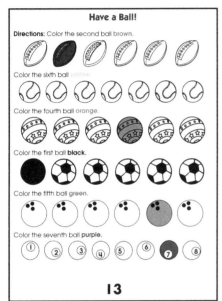

13

Which Place in the Race?

Directions: Write the correct word to tell each runner's place in the race.

fifth
first
fourth
third
seventh
second
sixth

14

How Many Robots in All?

Directions: Look at the pictures. Complete the addition sentences.

Example:
How many s are there in all?
2 + 4 = 6

How many s are there in all?
3 + 5 = 8

How many s are there in all?
4 + 3 = 7

How many s are there in all?
4 + 1 = 5

How many s are there in all?
2 + 5 = 7

How many s are there in all?
4 + 4 = 8

15

The Missing Chickens

Directions: Draw the missing pictures. Complete the addition sentences.

＋ ＝

＋ ＝

Example:
_1_ + 2 = 3

_3_ + 3 = 6

＋ ＝

＋ ＝

5 + _2_ = 7

_2_ + 3 = 5

＋ ＝

＋ ＝

_4_ + 4 = 8

7 + _1_ = 8

16

Counting Up

Directions: Count up to get the sum. Write the missing addend in each blank.

3 + _3_ = 6   8 + _1_ = 9
4 + _1_ = 5   4 + _2_ = 6
7 + _2_ = 9   6 + _0_ = 6
2 + _2_ = 4   5 + _2_ = 7
3 + _5_ = 8   4 + _3_ = 7
5 + _0_ = 5   9 + _1_ = 10
8 + _2_ = 10   5 + _3_ = 8
7 + _1_ = 8   7 + _3_ = 10
6 + _3_ = 9   6 + _2_ = 8

17

Coloring by Number

Directions: Find each sum.
If the sum is **13**, color the space brown.
If the sum is **14**, color the space yellow.
If the sum is **16**, color the space red.
If the sum is **17**, color the space blue.

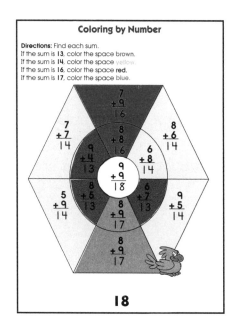

18

Problem Solving

Directions: Solve each problem.

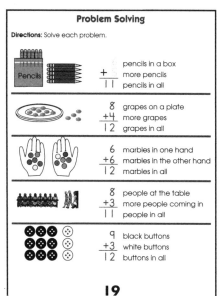

$\begin{array}{r} \\ + \\ \hline 11 \end{array}$	pencils in a box more pencils pencils in all
$\begin{array}{r} 8 \\ +4 \\ \hline 12 \end{array}$	grapes on a plate more grapes grapes in all
$\begin{array}{r} 6 \\ +6 \\ \hline 12 \end{array}$	marbles in one hand marbles in the other hand marbles in all
$\begin{array}{r} 8 \\ +3 \\ \hline 11 \end{array}$	people at the table more people coming in people in all
$\begin{array}{r} 9 \\ +3 \\ \hline 12 \end{array}$	black buttons white buttons buttons in all

19

Hop Along Numbers

Directions: Use the number line to count back.

Example: 8, _7_ , _6_

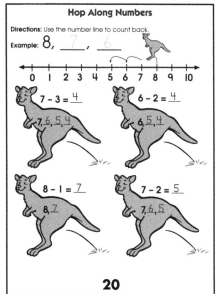

$7 - 3 = \underline{4}$
7, 6, 5, 4

$6 - 2 = \underline{4}$
6, 5, 4

$8 - 1 = \underline{7}$
8, 7

$7 - 2 = \underline{5}$
7, 6, 5

20

Leaves Leaving the Limb

Directions: Subtract to find the difference. Use the code to color the leaves. Code: **0 = green   1 = red   2 = yellow   3 = brown**

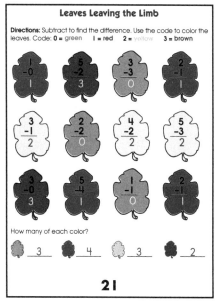

How many of each color?

🍃 _3_   🍂 _4_   🍃 _3_   🍀 _2_

21

Secrets of Subtraction

Directions: Solve the subtraction problems. Use the code to find the secret message.

Code:
7	5	2	6	4	3
K	T	Y	E	W	A

PLEASE, DON'T EVER

8	10	9	10		9	6	7	8
-3	-7	-2	-4		-6	-2	-4	-6
5	3	7	6		3	4	3	2
T	A	K	E		A	W	A	Y

MY MATH!

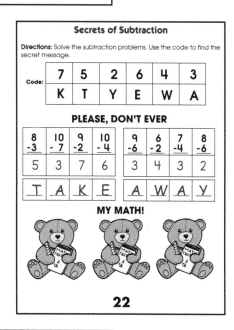

22

Subtraction Fun

Directions: Subtract to find each difference.

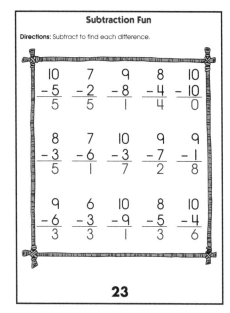

10 −5 5	7 −2 5	9 −8 1	8 −4 4	10 −10 0
8 −3 5	7 −6 1	10 −3 7	9 −7 2	9 −1 8
9 −6 3	6 −3 3	10 −9 1	8 −5 3	10 −4 6

23

Subtraction Facts Through 18

Directions: Subtract.
Example:

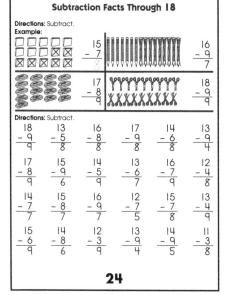

15 −7 8		16 −9 7
17 −8 9		18 −9 9

Directions: Subtract.

18 −9 9	13 −5 8	16 −8 8	17 −9 8	14 −6 8	13 −9 4
17 −8 9	15 −9 6	14 −5 9	13 −6 7	16 −7 9	12 −4 8
14 −7 7	15 −8 7	16 −9 7	12 −7 5	15 −7 8	13 −4 9
15 −6 9	14 −8 6	12 −3 9	13 −9 4	14 −9 5	11 −3 8

24

Math: Grade 2

"Grrreat" Picture

Directions: Subtract. Write the answer in the space. Then, color the spaces according to the answers.

1 = white   2 = purple   3 = black   4 = green   5 = white
6 = blue   7 = pink   8 = gray   9 = orange   10 = red

25

Facts for 10

Directions: Add or subtract.

Examples:

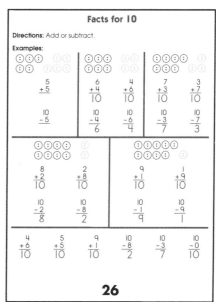

5 +5 = 10	6 +4 = 10	4 +6 = 10	7 +3 = 10	3 +7 = 10
10 −5 = 5	10 −4 = 6	10 −6 = 4	10 −3 = 7	10 −7 = 3

8 +2 = 10	2 +8 = 10	9 +1 = 10	1 +9 = 10
10 −2 = 8	10 −8 = 2	10 −1 = 9	10 −9 = 1

4 +6 = 10	5 +5 = 10	9 +1 = 10	10 −8 = 2	10 −3 = 7	10 −0 = 10

26

Addition and Subtraction Fun

Directions: Solve the number problem under each picture. Write + or − to show if you should add or subtract.

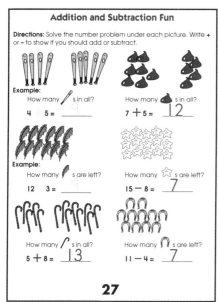

Example:
How many ✏s in all?
4 + 5 = ___

How many ♥s in all?
7 + 5 = 12

Example:
How many 🪶s are left?
12 − 3 = ___

How many ☆s are left?
15 − 8 = 7

How many 🦯s in all?
5 + 8 = 13

How many ⊔s are left?
11 − 4 = 7

27

Big Families

Directions: Complete each number sentence in each number family.

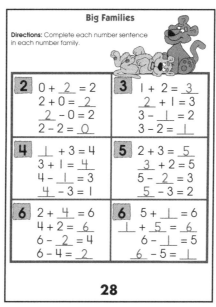

2
0 + 2 = 2
2 + 0 = 2
2 − 0 = 2
2 − 2 = 0

3
1 + 2 = 3
2 + 1 = 3
3 − 1 = 2
3 − 2 = 1

4
1 + 3 = 4
3 + 1 = 4
4 − 1 = 3
4 − 3 = 1

5
2 + 3 = 5
3 + 2 = 5
5 − 2 = 3
5 − 3 = 2

6
2 + 4 = 6
4 + 2 = 6
6 − 2 = 4
6 − 4 = 2

6
5 + 1 = 6
1 + 5 = 6
6 − 1 = 5
6 − 5 = 1

28

Place Value: Ones, Tens

The **place value** of a digit or numeral is shown by where it is in the number. For example, in the number **23**, **2** has the place value of **tens**, and **3** is **ones**.

Directions: Add the tens and ones and write your answers in the blanks.

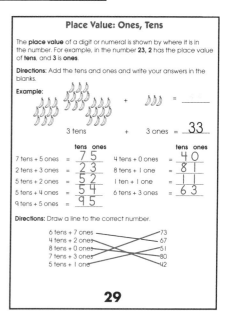

Example:
3 tens + 3 ones = 33

	tens ones		tens ones
7 tens + 5 ones =	7 5	4 tens + 0 ones =	4 0
2 tens + 3 ones =	2 3	8 tens + 1 one =	8 1
5 tens + 2 ones =	5 2	1 ten + 1 one =	1 1
5 tens + 4 ones =	5 4	6 tens + 3 ones =	6 3
9 tens + 5 ones =	9 5		

Directions: Draw a line to the correct number.

6 tens + 7 ones — 73
4 tens + 2 ones — 67
8 tens + 0 ones — 51
7 tens + 3 ones — 80
5 tens + 1 one — 42

29

Numbers 11 Through 18

1¢   10¢   10¢

Directions: Complete the problems.

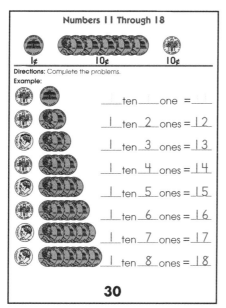

Example:
___ ten ___ one = ___
1 ten 2 ones = 12
1 ten 3 ones = 13
1 ten 4 ones = 14
1 ten 5 ones = 15
1 ten 6 ones = 16
1 ten 7 ones = 17
1 ten 8 ones = 18

30

Numbers 40 Through 99

Directions: Complete the problems.

Example:

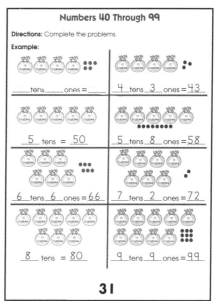

___ tens ___ ones = ___	4 tens 3 ones = 43
5 tens = 50	5 tens 8 ones = 58
6 tens 6 ones = 66	7 tens 2 ones = 72
8 tens = 80	9 tens 9 ones = 99

31

Hundreds, Tens, and Ones

Directions: Count the groups of crayons. Write the number of hundreds, tens, and ones.

Example:

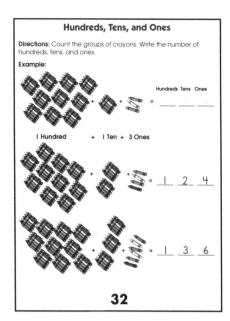

Hundreds Tens Ones

1 Hundred + 1 Ten + 3 Ones

= 1 2 4

= 1 3 6

32

Count 'Em Up!

Directions: Look at the example. Then, write the missing numbers in the blanks.

Example:

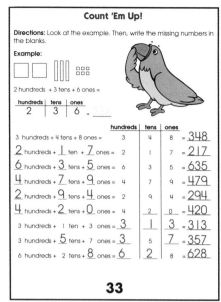

2 hundreds + 3 tens + 6 ones =

hundreds	tens	ones
2	3	6	= 236

	hundreds	tens	ones	
3 hundreds + 4 tens + 8 ones =	3	4	8	= 348
2 hundreds + 1 ten + 7 ones =	2	1	7	= 217
6 hundreds + 3 tens + 5 ones =	6	3	5	= 635
4 hundreds + 7 tens + 9 ones =	4	7	9	= 479
2 hundreds + 9 tens + 4 ones =	2	9	4	= 294
4 hundreds + 2 tens + 0 ones =	4	2	0	= 420
3 hundreds + 1 ten + 3 ones =	3	1	3	= 313
3 hundreds + 5 tens + 7 ones =	3	5	7	= 357
6 hundreds + 2 tens + 8 ones =	6	2	8	= 628

33

Place Value: Thousands

Directions: Study the example. Write the missing numbers.

Example:

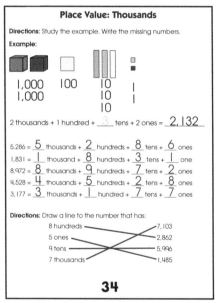

1,000	100	10	1
1,000		10	1
		10	

2 thousands + 1 hundred + 3 tens + 2 ones = 2,132

5,286 = 5 thousands + 2 hundreds + 8 tens + 6 ones
1,831 = 1 thousand + 8 hundreds + 3 tens + 1 one
8,972 = 8 thousands + 9 hundreds + 7 tens + 2 ones
4,528 = 4 thousands + 5 hundreds + 2 tens + 8 ones
3,177 = 3 thousands + 1 hundred + 7 tens + 7 ones

Directions: Draw a line to the number that has:

8 hundreds — 7,103
5 ones — 2,862
9 tens — 5,996
7 thousands — 1,485

34

Adding Tens

3 tens	30	6 tens	60
+ 4 tens	+40	+ 2 tens	+20
7 tens	70	tens	

Directions: Add.

2 tens	20	6 tens	60
+ 4 tens	+40	+ 2 tens	+20
6 tens	60	8 tens	80

20	10	40	30	50
+20	+50	+20	+40	+30
40	60	60	70	80

30	60	20	70	10
+20	+10	+50	+10	+10
50	70	70	80	20

10	40	80	60	20
+20	+40	+10	+30	+60
30	80	90	90	80

70	40	30	50	30
+20	+10	+10	+40	+30
90	50	40	90	60

35

2-Digit Addition

Directions: Study the example. Follow the steps to add.

Example: 33
+41

Step 1: Add the ones.

Step 2: Add the tens.

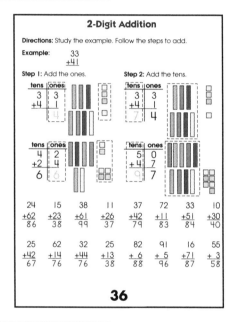

tens	ones
3	3
+4	1
	4

tens	ones
3	3
+4	1
7	4

tens	ones
4	2
+2	4
6	6

tens	ones
5	0
+4	7
9	7

24	15	38	11	37	72	33	10
+62	+23	+61	+26	+42	+11	+51	+30
86	38	99	37	79	83	84	40

25	62	32	25	82	91	16	55
+42	+14	+44	+13	+ 6	+ 5	+71	+ 3
67	76	76	38	88	96	87	58

36

Prehistoric Problems

Directions: Solve the subtraction problems. Use the code to color the picture.

Code:
25 = blue   57 = green
31 = yellow   14 = orange
21 = brown   11 = red

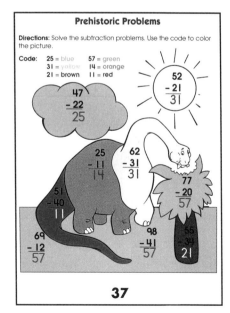

52
- 21
31

47
- 22
25

25
- 11
14

62
- 31
31

77
- 20
57

51
- 40
11

69
- 12
57

98
- 41
57

55
- 34
21

37

2-Digit Addition

Directions: Add the ones.   Rename 15 as 10 + 5.   Add the tens.

56   6
+29   9
          15 or 10 + 5

56
+29
  5

56
+29
8 5

Directions: Add the ones.   Rename 12 as 10 + 2.   Add the tens.

47   7
+35   5
          12 or 10 + 2

47
+35
  2

47
+35
8 2

Directions: Add.

Examples:

45	13	48	69	54
+28	+19	+35	+18	+39
		83	87	93

44	37	28	73	66
+17	+18	+36	+18	+29
61	55	64	91	95

52	38	64	29	75
+39	+47	+18	+45	+17
91	85	82	74	92

38

2-Digit Subtraction: Regrouping

Subtraction is "taking away" or subtracting one number from another to find the difference. Regrouping is using **one ten** to form **ten ones**, **one 100** to form **ten tens**, and so on.

Directions: Study the examples. Follow the steps to subtract.

Example: 37
          -19

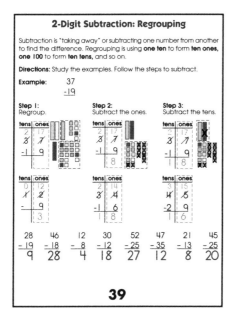

28	46	12	30	52	47	21	45
-19	-18	-8	-12	-25	-35	-13	-25
9	28	4	18	27	12	8	20

39

Addition and Subtraction Review

Directions: Add.

4	8	9	7	5	6
+9	+6	+8	+6	+7	+5
13	14	17	13	12	11

9	5	7	9	8	7
+6	+8	+4	+9	+7	+9
15	13	11	18	15	16

30	20	45	52	60	83
+40	+30	+23	+23	+25	+15
70	50	68	75	85	98

Directions: Subtract.

16	15	13	12	11	17
-7	-9	-4	-7	-9	-8
9	6	9	5	2	9

18	17	16	15	4	16
-9	-9	-8	-8	-7	-9
9	8	8	7	7	7

40	60	85	73	96	54
-30	-10	-23	-41	-43	-44
10	50	62	32	53	10

40

Adding Hundreds

Examples:

5 hundreds	500	4 hundreds	400
+ 3 hundreds	+ 300	+ 5 hundreds	+ 500
8 hundreds	800	hundreds	

Directions: Add.

3 hundreds	300	6 hundreds	600
+ 1 hundreds	+ 100	+ 2 hundreds	+ 200
hundreds		8 hundreds	800

200	100	600	400
+ 200	+ 700	+ 300	+ 500
400	800	900	900

300	800	400	700
+ 400	+ 100	+ 400	+ 200
700	900	800	900

500	100	500	300
+ 100	+ 600	+ 200	+ 200
600	700	700	500

300	400	300	200
+ 300	+ 200	+ 500	+ 100
600	600	800	300

41

3-Digit Addition

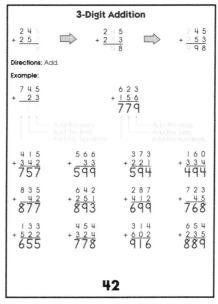

Directions: Add.

Example:

745	623
+ 23	+ 156
	779

415	566	373	160
+ 342	+ 33	+ 221	+ 334
757	599	594	494

835	642	287	723
+ 42	+ 251	+ 412	+ 45
877	893	699	768

133	454	314	654
+ 522	+ 324	+ 602	+ 235
655	778	916	889

42

Subtracting Hundreds

8 hundreds	800	6 hundreds	600
- 3 hundreds	- 300	- 2 hundreds	- 200
5 hundreds	500	hundreds	

Directions: Subtract.

Example:

9 hundreds	900	3 hundreds	300
- 7 hundreds	- 700	- 1 hundreds	- 100
hundreds		2 hundreds	200

700	500	900	800
- 300	- 400	- 400	- 500
400	100	500	300

600	300	500	400
- 500	- 200	- 100	- 200
100	100	400	200

900	800	600	500
- 100	- 400	- 200	- 300
800	400	400	200

400	700	800	900
- 100	- 600	- 200	- 600
300	100	600	300

43

Problem Solving

Directions: Solve each problem.

Example:

The grocery store buys 568 cans of beans.
It sells 345 cans of beans.
How many cans of beans are left?

The cooler holds 732 gallons of milk.
It has 412 gallons of milk in it.
How many more gallons of milk will it take to fill the cooler?

732
- 412
320

Ann does 635 push-ups.
Carl does 421 push-ups.
How many more push-ups does Ann do?

635
- 421
214

Kurt has 386 pennies.
Neal has 32 pennies.
How many more pennies does Kurt have?

386
- 32
354

It takes 874 nails to build a tree house.
Jillian has 532 nails.
How many more nails does she need?

874
- 532
342

44

Multiplication

Multiplication is a short way to find the sum of adding the same number a certain amount of times. For example, 7 x 4 = 28 instead of 7 + 7 + 7 + 7 = 28.

Directions: Study the example. Solve the problems.

Example:

3 + 3 + 3 = 9
3 threes = 9
3 x 3 = 9

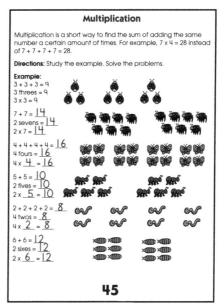

7 + 7 = 14
2 sevens = 14
2 x 7 = 14

4 + 4 + 4 + 4 = 16
4 fours = 16
4 x 4 = 16

5 + 5 = 10
2 fives = 10
2 x 5 = 10

2 + 2 + 2 + 2 = 8
4 twos = 8
4 x 2 = 8

6 + 6 = 12
2 sixes = 12
2 x 6 = 12

45

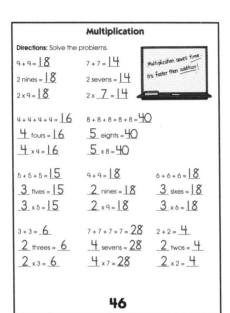

Multiplication

Directions: Solve the problems.

Multiplication saves time. It's faster than addition!

$9 + 9 = 18$ $7 + 7 = 14$

2 nines = 18   2 sevens = 14

$2 \times 9 = 18$ $2 \times 7 = 14$

$4 + 4 + 4 + 4 = 16$ $8 + 8 + 8 + 8 + 8 = 40$

4 fours = 16   5 eights = 40

$4 \times 4 = 16$ $5 \times 8 = 40$

$5 + 5 + 5 = 15$ $9 + 9 = 18$ $6 + 6 + 6 = 18$

3 fives = 15   2 nines = 18   3 sixes = 18

$3 \times 5 = 15$ $2 \times 9 = 18$ $3 \times 6 = 18$

$3 + 3 = 6$ $7 + 7 + 7 + 7 = 28$ $2 + 2 = 4$

2 threes = 6   4 sevens = 28   2 twos = 4

$2 \times 3 = 6$ $4 \times 7 = 28$ $2 \times 2 = 4$

46

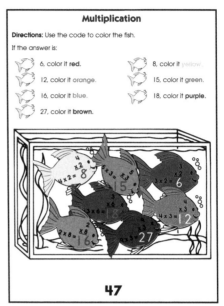

Multiplication

Directions: Use the code to color the fish.

If the answer is:

6, color it **red.**   8, color it yellow

12, color it orange.   15, color it **green.**

16, color it blue.   18, color it **purple.**

27, color it **brown.**

47

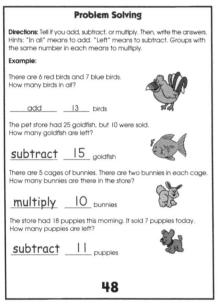

Problem Solving

Directions: Tell if you add, subtract, or multiply. Then, write the answers. Hints: "In all" means to add. "Left" means to subtract. Groups with the same number in each means to multiply.

Example:

There are 6 red birds and 7 blue birds.
How many birds in all?

_____add_____ _____13_____ birds

The pet store had 25 goldfish, but 10 were sold.
How many goldfish are left?

subtract 15 goldfish

There are 5 cages of bunnies. There are two bunnies in each cage.
How many bunnies are there in the store?

multiply 10 bunnies

The store had 18 puppies this morning. It sold 7 puppies today.
How many puppies are left?

subtract 11 puppies

48

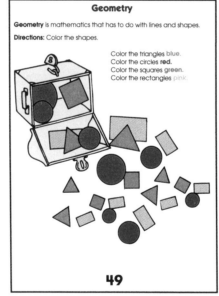

Geometry

Geometry is mathematics that has to do with lines and shapes.

Directions: Color the shapes.

Color the triangles blue.
Color the circles **red.**
Color the squares **green.**
Color the rectangles pink.

49

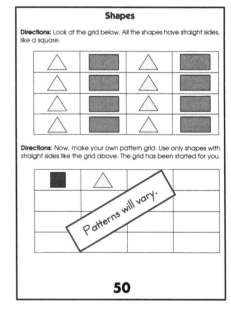

Shapes

Directions: Look at the grid below. All the shapes have straight sides, like a square.

Directions: Now, make your own pattern grid. Use only shapes with straight sides like the grid above. The grid has been started for you.

Patterns will vary.

50

Measurement: Inches

An **inch** is a unit of length in the standard measurement system.

Directions: Use the ruler on pg. 203 to measure each object to the nearest inch.

Example: The paper clip is about 1 inch long.

1 inch

about __1__ inches

about __1__ inches

about __4__ inches

about __2__ inches

about __2__ inches

about __4__ inches

about __3__ inches

51

Measuring in Centimeters

Directions: Use a centimeter ruler to find the height or the length of the objects below. Write the answer in each blank.

Example:

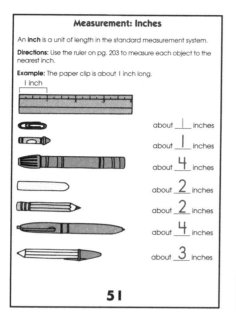

14 cm

centimeters

12 cm

20 cm

6 cm

6 cm

3 cm

52

What a Meal!

Directions: Use the pictograph to complete each sentence below.

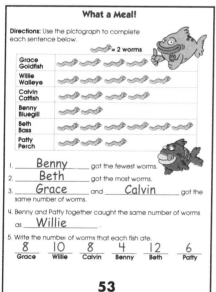

= 2 worms

Grace Goldfish	
Willie Walleye	
Calvin Catfish	
Benny Bluegill	
Beth Bass	
Patty Perch	

1. __Benny__ got the fewest worms.
2. __Beth__ got the most worms.
3. __Grace__ and __Calvin__ got the same number of worms.
4. Benny and Patty together caught the same number of worms as __Willie__.
5. Write the number of worms that each fish ate.

8	10	8	4	12	6
Grace	Willie	Calvin	Benny	Beth	Patty

53

Graphs

Directions: Count the banana peels in each column. Color the boxes to show how many bananas have been eaten by the monkeys.

Example:

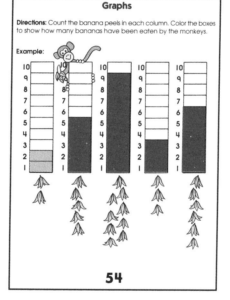

54

Treasure Quest

Directions: Read the directions. Draw the pictures where they belong on the grid. Start at 0 and go . . .

over 2, up 5. Draw a

over 9, up 3. Draw a

over 8, up 6. Draw a

over 5, up 2. Draw a

over 1, up 7. Draw a

over 7, up 1. Draw a

over 6, up 4. Draw a

over 2, up 3. Draw a

over 3, up 1. Draw a

over 4, up 6. Draw a

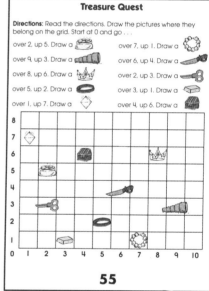

55

Thirds and Fourths

Directions: Each shape has **3** equal parts. Color one section, or $\frac{1}{3}$, of each shape.

Directions: Each shape has **4** equal parts. Color one section, or $\frac{1}{4}$, of each shape.

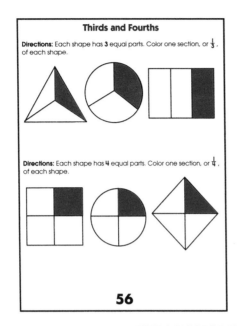

Fractions: Half, Third, Fourth

Directions: Color the correct fraction of each shape.

Examples:

shaded part 1
equal parts 2
$\frac{1}{2}$ (one-half)

shaded part 1
equal parts 3
$\frac{1}{3}$ (one-third)

shaded part 1
equal parts 4
$\frac{1}{4}$ (one-fourth)

Color $\frac{1}{3}$ red

Color $\frac{1}{4}$ blue

Color $\frac{1}{2}$ orange

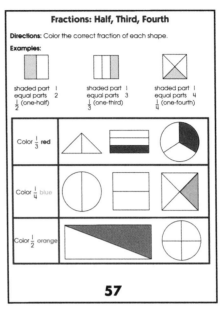

56

57

Fractions: Half, Third, Fourth

Directions: Study the examples. Circle the fraction that shows the shaded part. Then, circle the fraction that shows the white part.

Examples:

shaded   white
$\frac{1}{4}$ $\frac{1}{3}$ $\frac{1}{2}$ $\frac{1}{3}$ $\frac{1}{2}$ $\frac{1}{4}$

shaded   white
$\frac{1}{2}$ $\frac{2}{2}$ $\frac{3}{3}$ $\frac{2}{3}$ $\frac{2}{2}$ $\frac{3}{4}$

shaded   white
$\frac{1}{4}$ $\frac{1}{2}$ $\frac{3}{4}$ $\frac{1}{4}$ $\frac{2}{3}$ $\frac{1}{2}$

shaded   white
$\frac{1}{4}$ $\frac{1}{3}$ $\frac{1}{2}$

shaded   white
$\frac{2}{4}$ $\frac{2}{3}$ $\frac{2}{2}$

shaded   white
$\frac{3}{4}$ $\frac{1}{3}$ $\frac{3}{3}$

shaded   white
$\frac{1}{2}$ $\frac{1}{4}$ $\frac{1}{3}$

shaded   white
$\frac{2}{3}$ $\frac{2}{4}$ $\frac{2}{2}$ $\frac{1}{3}$ $\frac{2}{4}$ $\frac{2}{2}$

shaded   white
$\frac{1}{3}$ $\frac{2}{4}$ $\frac{2}{2}$ $\frac{1}{2}$ $\frac{1}{4}$ $\frac{1}{3}$

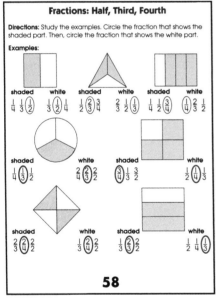

Writing the Time

An hour is sixty minutes long. It takes an hour for the BIG HAND to go around the clock. When the BIG HAND is on 12, and the little hand points to a number, that is the hour!

Directions: The **BIG HAND** is on the **12**. Color it red. The **little hand** is on the **8**. Color it blue.

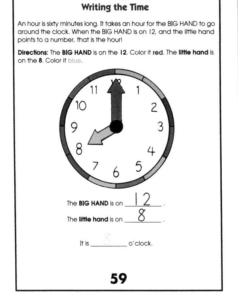

The **BIG HAND** is on 12 .
The **little hand** is on 8 .

It is _____ o'clock.

Writing the Time

Directions: Color the little hour hand **red**. Fill in the blanks.

The **BIG HAND** is on 12 .
The **little hand** is on 3 .

It is 3 o'clock.

The **BIG HAND** is on 12 .
The **little hand** is on 6 .

It is 6 o'clock.

The **BIG HAND** is on 12 .
The **little hand** is on 1 .

It is 1 o'clock.

The **BIG HAND** is on 12 .
The **little hand** is on 10 .

It is 10 o'clock.

58

59

60

Matching Digital and Face Clocks

Long ago, there were only wind-up clocks. Today, we also have electric and battery clocks. We may soon have solar clocks!

Directions: Match the digital and face clocks that show the same time.

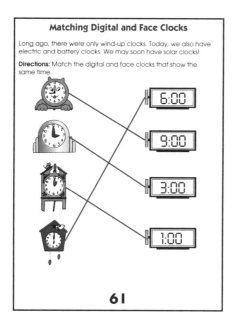

61

Writing Time on the Half-Hour

Directions: Write the times.

11:00
30 minutes past

Half-hour later

11:30
11 o'clock

1:00
30 minutes past

Half-hour later

1:30
1 o'clock

What is your dinner time?

Directions: Circle the time you eat.

4:30   Answers will vary.   7:30

o:30

62

Counting Pennies

Directions: Count the pennies. How many cents?

Example:

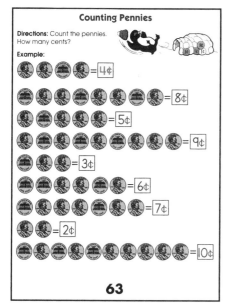

= 4¢

= 8¢

= 5¢

= 9¢

= 3¢

= 6¢

= 7¢

= 2¢

= 10¢

63

Nickels: Counting by Fives

Directions: Count the nickels by 5s. Write the amount.

Example:

5 cents = 1 nickel

15¢   10¢

Count 5, 10, 15   Count 5, 10

25¢   35¢

Count 5, 10, 15, 20, 25   Count 5, 10, 15, 20, 25, 30, 35

20¢   30¢

Count 5, 10, 15, 20.   Count 5, 10, 15, 20, 25, 30.

64

Dimes: Counting by Tens

Directions: Count by 10s. Write the number. Circle the group with more.

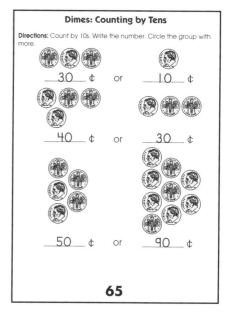

30¢   or   10¢

40¢   or   30¢

50¢   or   90¢

65

Counting With Dimes, Nickels, and Pennies

Directions: Count the money. Start with the dime. Write the amount.

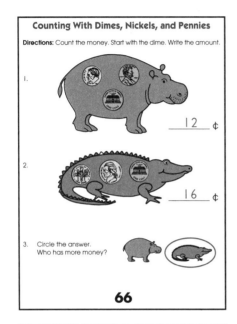

1. _12_ ¢

2. _16_ ¢

3. Circle the answer. Who has more money?

66

Counting With Quarters, Dimes, Nickels, and Pennies

Directions: Match the money with the amount.

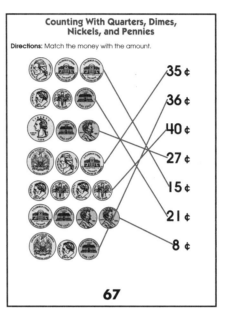

35 ¢
36 ¢
40 ¢
27 ¢
15 ¢
21 ¢
8 ¢

67

Making Exact Amounts of Money: Two Ways to Pay

Directions: Find two ways to pay. Show what coins you use.

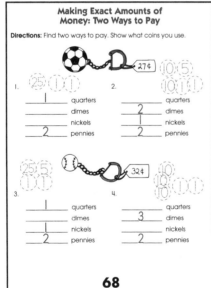

1.
_1_ quarters
___ dimes
___ nickels
_2_ pennies

2.
___ quarters
_2_ dimes
_1_ nickels
_2_ pennies

3.
_1_ quarters
___ dimes
_1_ nickels
_2_ pennies

4.
___ quarters
_3_ dimes
___ nickels
_2_ pennies

68

Making Exact Amounts of Money: How Much More?

Directions: Count the coins. Find out how much more money you need to pay the exact amount.

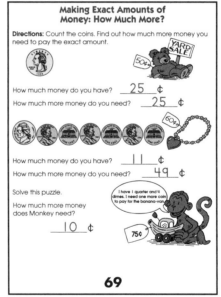

How much money do you have? _25_ ¢
How much more money do you need? _25_ ¢

How much money do you have? _11_ ¢
How much more money do you need? _49_ ¢

Solve this puzzle.

How much more money does Monkey need?

_10_ ¢

I have 1 quarter and 4 dimes. I need one more coin to pay for the banana-van.

75¢

69